Published by The Metropolitan Museum of Art and Skira Rizzoli Publications, Inc.

The Metropolitan Museum of Art
1000 Fifth Avenue
New York, NY 10028
212.570.3894
www.metmuseum.org

Skira Rizzoli Publications, Inc.
300 Park Avenue South
New York, NY 10010
www.rizzoliusa.com

Produced by the Department of Special Publications, The Metropolitan Museum of Art:
Robie Rogge, Publishing Manager; Mimi Tribble, Editor; Atif Toor, Designer, with Kate Kennedy;
Gillian J. Moran, Production. Photography by The Metropolitan Museum of Art Photograph Studio.

Printed in China
15 14 13 12 11   10 9 8 7 6 5 4 3 2 1

Distributed in the U. S. trade by Random House, New York

Library of Congress Control Number: 2011922125

ISBN-13: 978-1-58839-418-7 (MMA)
ISBN-13: 978-0-8478-3701-4 (Skira Rizzoli)

THE METROPOLITAN MUSEUM OF ART | NEW YORK

Skira *Rizzoli*
NEW YORK

A

is for **AVENUE.**

B

is for **BROOKLYN BRIDGE.**

C

is for **CENTRAL PARK.**

D

is for **DOCK.**

is for **EMPIRE STATE BUILDING.**

is for **FLATIRON BUILDING.**

G

is for **GRAND CENTRAL TERMINAL.**

is for **HARLEM.**

is for **ISLAND**.

J

is for **JEFFERSON MARKET.**

K

is for **KIDS.**

is for **LOWER EAST SIDE.**

is for **METROPOLITAN MUSEUM OF ART.**

is for **NEW YORK AT NIGHT.**

is for **ON STAGE.**

P

is for **PEOPLE.**

is for **QUEENSBORO BRIDGE.**

R

is for **ROCKEFELLER CENTER.**

S

is for **STATUE OF LIBERTY.**

T

is for **TIMES SQUARE.**

U

is for **UNION SQUARE.**

is for **VIEWS.**

W

is for **WALL STREET.**

is for **X**.

is for **YELLOW TAXI.**